It's NOT Your Fault

Patricia Reneé McGee-Martin

*Priority*ONE
publications
Detroit, MI USA

Copyright © 2024, 2025 Second Edition
by Patricia Reneé McGee-Martin

All rights reserved.
No part of this publication may be reproduced, distributed, or transmitted in any form or by any means, including photocopying, recording, or other electronic or mechanical methods, or conveyed via the internet or a website without the prior written permission of the publisher. Please direct all inquiries to:

PriorityONE Publications, LLC
P.O. Box 361332 | Grosse Pointe, MI 48236
E-mail: info@priorityonebooks.com
URL: http://www.priorityonebooks.com

ISBN 13: 978-1-933972-80-0
ISBN 10: 1-933972-80-7

Editing, Cover & Interior Design Artwork generated with the assistance of artificial intelligence and further edited by
Christina Dixon

Printed in the United States of America

DEDICATION

This book is dedicated to, first, God my Savior. The One who heals and delivers me from all hurt, harm and dangers. The one who heals my physical, mental and spiritual body.

Even though I have and may again, walked through the valley of darkness, I am never afraid because I know that He is with me in every situation.

Secondly, this book is dedicated to every person who has gone through any type of abuse. Know that God is with you. Even in the middle of the storm, God is with you and you will come out better than before. Have faith and believe that God will not forget you or leave you alone. God has a plan for your life that is bigger, better and stronger than anything the enemy can do to you.

And to my biggest fans and loves:
James Martin, Renee Muhammad, and
Denise (Nikki) Smith.

Remember Psalm 27:1:
The Lord is my light and my salvation, whom shall I fear? The Lord is the strength of my life,
of whom shall I be afraid?

A bad thing happened to you.
It's NOT your fault.

It happens to boys.

It happens to girls.

It happens to babies.

It happens to toddlers and pre-teens.

It happens to teenagers
and even adults.

The Bible says,
"When you go through deep waters, I will be with you. When you go through rivers of difficulty, you will not drown. When you walk through the fire of oppression, you will not be burned up; the flames will not consume you."
(NLT) Isaiah 43:2

Do you know what abuse is?
Abuse is when someone hurts you,
doesn't take care of you, or touches you
in a way that feels yucky or wrong.

It can be someone you know,
like a parent, teacher, or friend.
If that happens, always tell
a grown-up you trust.

* FACTS:
Your body belongs to you.
No-one should touch or see your body without a good reason.

* If a grown up or older child wants to touch or see your private parts or show you theirs, that's NOT OK.

* Even if it's someone you know, it's still NOT OK.

* You should tell someone straight away, even if they ask you to keep it a secret'.

You did nothing wrong.

It can happen to anyone.

It's NOT your fault.

It's okay to be sad.

It's okay to be mad.

But,

You must tell someone!

Tell a trusted adult.

You have choices.

A friendly police officer.

Grandparents.

A teacher you feel safe with.

A doctor.

You are a super kid.

Don't let bad things stop your life.
You can still be anything you want to be like an astronaut.

Or a baker...

Or a doctor...

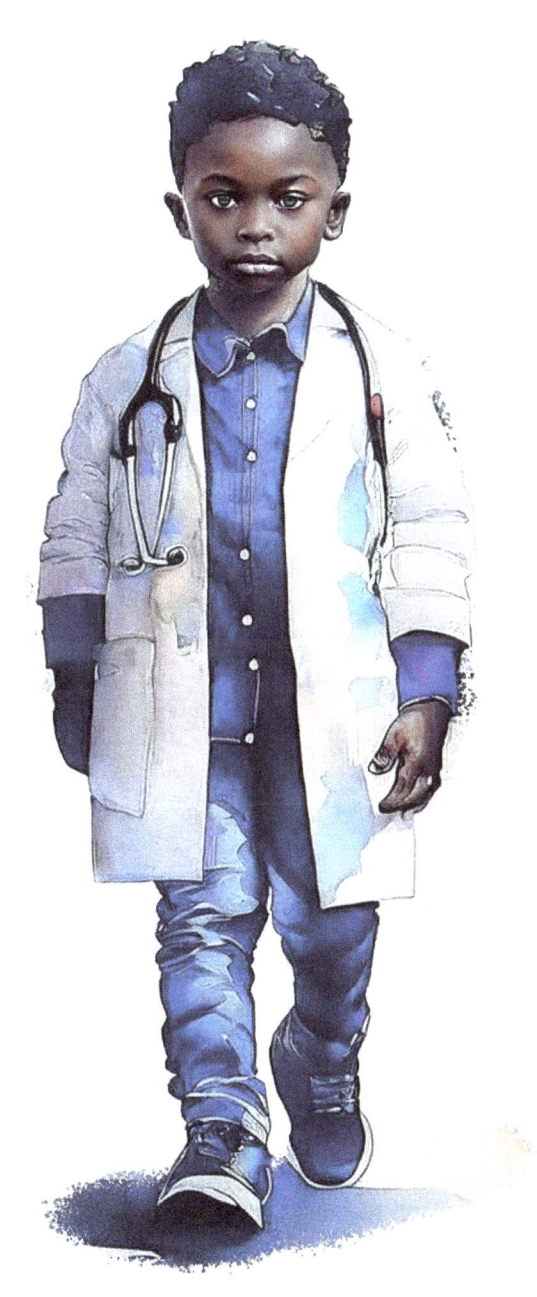

Or a judge...

Or a singer...

Or a pilot...

Or an engineer...

Or an artist...

Our Father in heaven,
Hallowed be Your name.

Your kingdom come,

Your will be done,

on earth as it is in heaven.

Give us today our daily bread.

And forgive us our debts,
as we also have forgiven our debtors.

And lead us not into temptation, but deliver us from the evil one.

For Thine is the kingdom,
and the power, and the glory,
forever. Amen.

You can do anything you want to do.
You can make it.
You are a super kid.
You have a future.
This bad thing does not define you.

PANTS Rule for Kids

 Private parts are private. No one is permitted to touch you without your permission.

 Always remember, your body belongs only to you. No one has a right to you.

 No means no. Say it loud. Don't give in to pressure.

 There are no secrets from parents. If anyone hurts you in any way, tell a trusted and responsible adult.

 Say something so that you can be safe, well, and whole.

Author unknown

Can you find all the words in this puzzle?

```
      A R N                    R C U
     Q H E A L              N Y J R T
   P K C P F C O        S O R B S E L
   L L B O L N P O T F O D A A O
   E S U R V I V E N D T I F C V
   H P Y T T E L L E N C K E H E
   W I N N E R V A R E O R T E R
     E T B R A E F A I D E Y R
     I X A P G G R P R F P Q J
     N T S U R T D F F U I
     U P A R E N T S S
     R O R R A M L
     S D N R Q
     E U G
     A
```

DOCTOR	HELP	SAFETY	TRUST
FEAR	LOVE	SUPERKID	WINNER
FRIEND	NURSE	SURVIVE	
GRANDPARENTS	PARENTS	TEACHER	
HEAL	REPORT	TELL	

40

Use these empty pages to draw something that makes you happy.

Dear God, Thank you for loving me.
Thank you for protecting me.
Thank you for providing for me.

Give me a forgiving heart, even for those who would hurt Your children. Help me if I see an enemy to run from danger.

Thank you for healing me.
I pray for safety for myself
and for all of Your children.
Please keep us safe from all harm.

Help me be brave enough to
tell someone when I feel
that I am in danger.
I pray all this in Jesus Name. Amen

Remember,

It's not your fault.

Be the best that you can be!!!

The winner is YOU!

www.ingramcontent.com/pod-product-compliance
Lightning Source LLC
Chambersburg PA
CBHW081503070526
44586CB00019B/2463